MW01235820

i swallowed the sun
black out poetry edition

i swallowed the sun - black out poetry edition

written and arranged
by angie allen

all rights reserved

ISBN: 9798725551587
cover art by pride nyasha
2021 copyright © angie allen

instagram @angie.l.allen
instagram @pride_nyasha

original sin publishing

for all sunflowers everywhere and especially my *son*flowers, *jude & noah.* like flowers to the sun you keep me in search of the light, xx.

if i have learned
anything it is this…

light is wherever you are.

contents

also by angie allen

seeing is everything
the girl unboxed

i swallowed the sun

black out poetry edition

by angie allen

in life i live quietly
in love i am a
c a c o p h o n y.

i swallowed the sun

there is beauty in
the abandoned
in a life half lived
in a heart half loved
in the letting go
in the open palms
in the reaching.

when the darkness
makes you feel like
prey

create your own
light, become your
own day.

i swallowed the sun

thoughts
of you spread like
w i l d f l o w e r s
beneath my
skin.

angie allen

l o v e is a shifting bridge.

STAR

angie allen

it takes thousands
of years for a star's
light to reach you
so all i ask is this...

be gentle with your light.

i swallowed the sun

some say i
am a tangled
mess of a woman
but have you, dare
i ask, seen the roots
of a tree?

angie allen

patience

for even noah
sent out the thing
with wings three
times until it carried
back hope within its beak.

i swallowed the sun

and sometimes we
must be both the
sun and the flower
both the light and
the house

to shine for ourselves
to shine by ourselves

knowing light always
finds its way home.

while i mourn
the death of all
i was never to be

i became

and my path
becomes *me.*

there is that one person
we are good with, that
small window where we
can be both *i* and *we*
individual and union
where we give of
ourselves completely
yet don't lose ourselves
entirely - it's that small
space between lost & found.

angie allen

we search the world over
for what is familiar
you know it to be true
and although my face
has never laid eyes
on you, my fingers have
touched the words your
lips have breathed and
they, my love, feel very
much like home to me.

i swallowed the sun

scars & flowers

proof that darkness
ends and our world
is filled with color
once again.

light always finds
a way of reaching us
if light can find its
way…we can too.

i swallowed the sun

you met me there
beyond skin

bare boned & leafless

holding branches of
truth like a crucifix
waist deep in holy ground
you simply saw the roots
of me while the rest were
waiting for the bloom.

we are what we
believe we are
our minds do not
differentiate between
the real or the fake
if we are dreaming
asleep or sleeping awake
it only believes what its
been told, so starve it or
feed it and…

watch yourself *wither* or
watch yourself *unfold*.

i swallowed the sun

be present with the
ones present with you.

angie allen

these small things
of which i write
are all things to me
both day and night.

just a little sunflower

there is just a little
sunflower at the
foot of my bed
only she looks like
the rising sun instead
her petals reach from
the east to the west
spreading light to all
before she rests.

angie allen

i feel you like
music in my
body, a symphony
under my skin,
a chorus of colors
just waiting to blend.

i swallowed the sun

like a bird
to its nest
i have flown

things with
wings have
a tendency
of migrating
home.

light is…*wherever* you are.

a seed lies entombed
the ground its cocoon
where the light is only
a night away to bloom
its wings before decay.

angie allen

a nuthatch made its
home in my dead
abandoned tree and
now tweets and sings
atop her lifeless branches
where the green leaves
used to breathe.

i swallowed the sun

there is something
special in the way
we can just 'be'
in this place where
i know you meets
you know me

there is no time
nor distance which
can ever separate that
for you see, we've created
light, and that shall travel
for all eternity.

whenever you are
near smiles appear :)

i swallowed the sun

in order to make
room for the light
we must let go of
what is keeping us
in its shadow.

skin & people

pieces (of ourselves)
we must shed
we must leave behind
to keep ourselves
w h o l e.

i swallowed the sun

if we were negated
by merely being
named then just think

of the many shapes of
y o u & m e

if we had been
named differently.

angie allen

we all bleed the same
when our hearts are
set aflame.

i swallowed the sun

absolute evergreen

is the color of
my love for you

never fading
always true.

they cannot hurt
what you do not
let in.

i swallowed the sun

it found me through
a hairline fracture
in my brokenness
and then… *there was*
light.

i have only ever felt
glimpsed, *never truly*
seen, just some version
of myself caught
somewhere in
b e t w e e n.

i swallowed the sun

RED GIANT

you are petals in
my memory
dried and pressed
hanging upside
down in some
dark corner of
my room.

i swallowed the sun

like watercolors…
bleed into me.

when the moon's light
waxes to new i am
reminded that even
light needs to rest
before it can wax
to full again too.

i swallowed the sun

do you hear that?
it is a goodly sound
the thunder of your
walls crashing

d
   o
     w
       n.

angie allen

the wind & you

things i throw
myself at rather
cautiously.

i swallowed the sun

how many times must
you look at me until i
look away, my eyes
screaming what my
tongue is too scared
to say?

angie allen

heat rises

and it's the
way you've
set my mind
ablaze that
has me
screaming

'fire.'

50

i swallowed the sun

i want to undress
your mind and get
to know the man
i want to touch you
in places never before
reached by hands

i want to be above you
i want to be below you
to be side-by-side
to be skin-to-skin

i want to really know you.

for me, it is not so much
about where i am going
it is more about where i
have been and how many
times i can bring myself
back.

i swallowed the sun

infinite

i am because you are
i will be because you
have been

to the many versions
of us there is seemingly
no end.

i want to know the
taste of your lips
the shape we take
with your hands on
my hips

i want to swim in
the stars of your skin
to taste the darkness
you hide within

to see if any of your
thoughts contain even
a small trace, just the
curve of my name.

i swallowed the sun

and there you were
an unexpected surprise
like a letter in the mail
or snowfall in july.

...where there are

wounds *there are*
also wings.

i swallowed the sun

in order to rise
you have to fall
and while some
falls break us they
don't end us

for where there are
wounds there are
also wings

it's not about how
long you stay down
it's about your ability
to rise from a fall then
spread your wings and
outshine them all.

angie allen

i close my eyes
thoughts run wild
we are more
legs than sheets
more tongues
than smiles
the weight of you
spilling over me
whilst our hips
move together
r   th   ca   y.
  hy   mi   l l

i swallowed the sun

this is the way

a cage for a bird
a lock and a key
without their
organized
'enlightenment'
i am actually free
the light was always
here...

shining inside of me.

angie allen

i love that place where
we undress one thought
at a time, clothes littering
the proverbial floors of
our minds

that place where we
talk ourselves empty
under foreign moons
where the unknown
is thick as scripture on
our hungry tongues

that place where we speak
liquid luminescence into
soft crescendoes until it
spills over the horizon
where the day of us is
stealing from the night of
us and i am fumbling for
the rewind button.

i swallowed the sun

there is nothing
quite like being
parted by a tongue
who knows how to
deftly bring honey
from its comb.

…his lips smacked of

hard-on poetry,
of friday 1 am *prose.*

i swallowed the sun

the devil went down to georgia
wore his halo in his eyes
hell bent on tasting heaven
in between my thighs
said, i heard you were an
angel once, he said, "yes
ma'am i'm afraid it's true
you see, it's just so hard not
to fall for pretty things like you."
his lips smacked of hard-on
poetry, of friday 1 am prose
as a sideways smile spread across
my lips and i leaned in really close
said, the apples in those lovely eyes
just reflect the others rotting at
your feet, the only one ripe for
plucking is the one between my teeth
i'm not like the others georgia boy
i like to be touched first without hands
enlighten me with your tongue and
i promise you'll find anything but
dry land.

angie allen

mirages & you

things just always
slightly out of reach
to the point of madness.

i swallowed the sun

i want to ride you like a storm
let the wind command our hips
crash over me, nothing lightly
blackened eyes, salted lips

press the thighs of me
onto you, nothing calm
nothing gentle please
take me like the night
in blinded ecstasy.

angie allen

liquid vowels
wanting lips
arched backs
limbs pressed
skin to skin
canvas divine
our tongues
repeating names
yours then *mine*
our bodies orchestrating
a symphony of skin
i no longer know where
you end and i begin.

i swallowed the sun

fire & legs

things that spread
when they have
completely lost
all control.

nature & mothers

things which always
find a way.

i swallowed the sun

we brought the energy
mixed our chemistry
our atoms blended
in absolute symmetry

with our hips in harmony
your lips stealing vowels
before they departed me

we unfolded like an
unchained melody
whilst falling from the
stars of our newly
formed galaxy.

she took a bite
her mind grew wings
a woman with sight
is a wondrous thing.

i swallowed the sun

glances, sex & smiles

things that are
best when given
s i d e w a y s.

angie allen

nude beginnings

i want to know
every inch of
your skin then
like strangers
begin again.

i swallowed the sun

drip club

you tasted of
life, and i?
i was thirsty.

73

angie allen

with just the tiniest
graze of your lips
against my skin
i felt winter fade
and summer's sun
pouring in.

i swallowed the sun

when it's sunny
or even when i'm blue
on the good days and
the really bad ones too
i always find i smile
whenever i think of you.

angie allen

…when my stomach growls

it's not from hunger, it's
the ghost of my words
starting to thunder.

i swallowed the sun

for you my tongue
still holds the words
i'd say if i were bold

run away with me
stay with me
spend the rest of
your days with me

instead they slip off the
edges and slide down
my throat, the walls of
my stomach they like to coat

when my stomach growls
it's not from hunger, it's
the ghost of my words
starting to thunder

wanting escape
wanting release
from this graveyard of
unspoken words that
i speak.

angie allen

surely there exists
between the something
and the nothing, a r t

to know this place is
to be inside the mind
of god.

78

i swallowed the sun

SUPERNOVA

your touch awakened
places in me i thought
were beyond reach
and yet, i ask…

*is there anywhere light
cannot travel?*

i swallowed the sun

it is, after all, religion
that keeps us going and
by religion i mean the
things we devote ourselves to
and perhaps i am specifically
talking about *writing* and
more specifically, *about you.*

angie allen

there are some
people that burn
bright with us
for a time and
then flicker out
like a flame

wish them well
all the same.

i swallowed the sun

i, the flower
you, the bee
and yet with
the slightest
of touch you
have managed
to e x t r a c t

h   y
   o   e
      n

angie allen

when thoughts of
you rise like these
georgia sunset skies
it makes my body
burn as if it were
meant to catch fire.

i swallowed the sun

.

i find our words
are braided with
seasons and time
falls between us
like leaves

subtly
  colorfully
    gracefully.

angie allen

liquid vowels and
muted howls, that's
what thoughts of
you are made of.

hearts & homes

places ghosts
haunt when
their people
are gone.

angie allen

winter has striped the
summer from the
branches of my skin
and i shall wait, for
in time nature tells
me i too will begin
again.

i swallowed the sun

no beau

there is silence
in my coffee
on my sheets
and in my skin
my body, a chorus
of hushed tones
my heart, a muted
violin.

angie allen

i am a chaser of light
sun by day and stars
by night

i am a lover of moments
the subtle and dim, the
ones where you peel
back the layers and
slowly let me in

i am a healer of hurts
and a writer of wrongs
and i'm awfully fond of
taking the long way home

and forgive me, but it's
true, taking the long way
home, you see, led me
straight to you.

i swallowed the sun

your hands, my hips
my teeth, your lips
things that fit rather
perfectly within our
grip.

angie allen

watching the sun set
tasting night fall
drinking & thinking
(of you)

nothing new, no nothing
new about this at all.

i swallowed the sun

eve

one woman walked
this earth nameless
legs rich with meaning

more savior
than woman
more hunger
than human

it was in the later
where she crossed
a line, overcome
with hunger she
ate to open her mind

and her name was
finally given to her
a gift written in
the sands of time.

angie allen

men
are like mountains
their beauty is in their strength
and yet when the earth of us moves beneath them
even the strongest cannot help but tremble at our touch.

i swallowed the sun

you've a heart that's
been half loved and
i've a life that's been
half lived

i figure together we
can make something
beautiful out of this.

angie allen

i will no longer be
branches outstretched
arms reaching with
nothing to touch.

the simple act of loving
you keeps me up at night
the simple act of wanting
you surrenders my body
without a fight

the simple act of this is not
so simple after all, you see
because me loving you and
wanting you will simply be
the end of all of me.

me | you

the truth is you were
standing in the way of
the light and i heard
nature whisper, 'there is
always another way'

and it was in that
moment i realized
if a way could not be
found it could be made
and i did...i made my
own way out

if nature can make her
way through, i could make
mine too...to another me
on the other side of you.

i swallowed the sun

sometimes i think
i could d   into an
ocean   i   of you
drown   v   and
never   e   fully
reach bottom.

angie allen

to me he is
but a mosaic
with soul
a mess of a
man, a little
more broken
a lot less whole.

i swallowed the sun

mouth opens just
enough for earth to
spill from our tongue

breathing
sound into words
strumming
song into chords
keeping
it on acoustic.

angie allen

i say your name like
a promise, a prayer,
a refrain, i carry it
an olive branch between
my ribs which cage the
expanse of what i feel for
you

i am a promise which doesn't
flood you (too much) but like
the second creative day issues
forth light previously cocooned
in the belly of darkness
now released like an invitation
to this holy land

take off your sandals, the shoes
of you and let's stand before one
another as bare boned walkers in
the wilderness of truth

it is there where i breathe you in
your manna skin and sampson hair
press scripture to our hips, offerings
of honey and of milk we, the
sacrificial rebels wrecked on the
unchurched shores somewhere
east of eden.

i swallowed the sun

when his heart
beat against mine
in that moment
we were simply
music.

angie allen

my hunger is hot
my faith is cold
and my feet are
tired from standing
on the truth.

i swallowed the sun

flowers, life & love

over before it ends
starts before it begins.

angie allen

it's not a question
of worth, rather
questioning if
what is worthy will
ever find me…

and stay.

106

beside myself

if only i could wake
up next to you, fill
the gaps in time
you'd be right beside
me and not just beside
me in my mind.

music playing
the candles lit
you touching me
with your fingertips
your breath on my
neck and my lips
on yours and we've
nothing but time and
each others skin to
explore.

i swallowed the sun

for even light was
born out of the belly
of darkness and made
its way to the other side.

event horizon

meet me there at that place
where ocean meets sky
where time stands still and
love never says goodbye.

i swallowed the sun

origin

it's really quite simple you see
adam is you and eve is me
we each have a beginning
a garden and a tree

there is an origin of us, a point
of no return, an apple bitten
from which we cannot run
from the path of who we will
become, the beginning is the
ending before the ending is
undone

free will is an illusion to make
us believe we are in control of
our destinies, but the truth is we
are never free in what we want
and that is what will eventually
haunt the halls…

a paradise lost with nobody home.

angie allen

sweet heat

it was my eyes
that gave me away
speaking the words
my mouth wouldn't say
how i wanted you in
the worst possible way
more tongue than words
more skin than clothes
guess that's the way
our story goes

a cupcake sweet
some bourbon neat
a brief moment in
the summer heat.

i swallowed the sun

i have no need to hide
from the mirror inside
all i need is paper and
pen, then a door opens...

oh, won't you come in?

angie allen

completely divine
your skin on mine
our wet mouths open
like day to night
the taste of summer
on your tongue before
it melts into the sky

no walls, no ceiling
no words, just feeling

of december peeling
from my bones as vowels
echo back the sounds
of our moans.

i swallowed the sun

we riot the night
before it bleeds
to day, with hands

t o g e t h e r

and no will left to

p r a y.

you are the ink
beneath my skin
the words on my
tongue before
they are penned.

i swallowed the sun

at first glance i seem
like a run on sentence

and yet if i were rain
i would be a storm
if i were water
i would be an ocean

if you were moses you
could not part the red
from the sea of me, for
i cannot be held back
(when it comes to you)

i will crash over you
i will flood you, i am
more water than woman
and therefore i must flow.

angie allen

throwing petals
so that even
in death *may*
we yet bloom
a g a i n.

i swallowed the sun

BLACK HOLE

angie allen

i wonder if the
catcher in the rye
was simply a
rabbit hole in
the sky

to get us to fall
alive with wings
tasting all of the
dangerous and
forbidden things

apples
the red pill
poison
you

fall with me and
taste them too, for
the catcher in the
rye is me, the
catcher in the
rye is you.

i swallowed the sun

i am everyone i have ever
loved and lost, i am every
place i have ever lived
and left, i am every season
that comes and goes, i am
all of these pieces and these
pieces become…

my *poetry* and my *prose*.

...i warned you,

these butterflies *inside*
flitting their wings
unleash disasters on
beautiful things.

i swallowed the sun

forgive me if i love you
just a little too hard
you should probably
know there are
hurricanes in my hips
tornadoes in my veins
when my mouth opens on
yours surely we would
unleash a fury that would
put a wildfire to shame
i warned you, these butterflies
inside flitting their wings
unleash disasters on beautiful
things, and yet something tells
me you won't mind a force
which needs a little reckoning.

angie allen

my
heart
b a r e s
marks and marks
and marks like a tree
all the days you've
been missing
from
me.

some want flesh
others want bone

this body comes
with both and if
you're not ready
for that then with
all due respect…

leave me the fuck alone.

angie allen

truth

depends on the
tongue telling it
and the medium
selling it.

i swallowed the sun

and if this is all
i am ever promised
these moments i have
spent here with you
please know it was
enough to have seen
me through, for these
words were mostly, if
not entirely, meant
for you.

angie allen

anywhere but here they say
and yet, isn't there just the other
side of here? you don't get there
without first being here and you
only get here coming from there,
don't you see?

perhaps they are the same
two sides of a linear coin

neither here nor there

here is only t(here) one letter
removed and yet still…i'd gladly
take there

because it is *anywhere but here.*

i swallowed the sun

haunted by all
we'll never be
the ghost of you
the ghost of me

here's a toast to
you, a toast to me,
a toast to the ghosts
we shall never be.

angie allen

the day b r e a k s

and night f
         a
         l
         l
         s

turns out it was
never about being
whole after all.

i swallowed the sun

sinulated reality

part of me wonders
if eve ate the fruit and
died and now we are
living in the reality of
a lie.

angie allen

no vacancy

hungry hearts
haunted minds
lonely things mask
shallow smiles

darkness spills
sadness calls
nobody home
here, *after all.*

i swallowed the sun

i wish dreams were
like a jukebox where
i could drop in a quarter
and play a song of a
time and a place where
i used to belong.

angie allen

…a lonely man with drinking hands

whose forty into his sixty
pulls a liquid trigger *on a*
priceless bottle of never ending
whisky.

i swallowed the sun

a lonely man with drinking hands
whose forty into his sixty
walks with ghosts, downing toasts
he builds bourbon bridges quickly

he's left behind, a void in time
their familiar was his home
he builds a bridge to get back to
them but they're long since dead
and gone

liquid loss comes with a cost
when loneliness is a friend
hellos and goodbyes
drinking buddy highs
he builds bourbon bridges quickly

a lonely man with drinking hands
whose forty into his sixty
pulls a liquid trigger on a priceless
bottle of never ending whisky.

angie allen

in a world of
flesh & bone
we are now
stars with skin

lights looking
for the shadows
of home.

if there is one thing
the ocean has taught
me it is this…

even water has a
b r e a k i n g point.

i was too much heart
and you were not
enough home and
yet still, for a time
we did create a
beautiful shelter...
didn't we?

i swallowed the sun

sunrise

with quiet house
and the love of
you still lighting
my skin, i rise.

there is something
breathtakingly
beautiful in that
which is caught
between this world
and the other
it's what i love about
something *wild*
it's what i love
about you.

i swallowed the sun

feed the hungry

it's what we have
done since the
beginning of time

men in gardens
babies in bellies

we feed that which
pangs with hunger.

you've ruined me
can't you see?

destruction has
never been worn
so beautifully.

i swallowed the sun

stare into the abyss
and it eventually
stares back at you
just means the darkness
in me is the darkness
in you

a face with familiar
eyes and we recognize
the view.

sunkissed

the sun is the
only thing to
have touched
my skin in days
and yet this too
is a reminder that
light always has a
way of touching us
in the places we
need it most.

i swallowed the sun

you're perfect
of the storm kind
the perfectly
unnorm kind.

angie allen

there was part of me that
understood even if i was
the catching type your
hands weren't exactly the
kind that held on.

i swallowed the sun

a rebel will always
rebel...only sheep
were meant for a fold.

i envy the velvet darkness
that falls upon his skin and
the soft hour that gently stirs
him before the day begins

i am jealous of the breeze
that dances through his hair
and the stars that fall from
the sky before his gazing stare

i would honestly be content,
i think, in simply breathing
the same air.

if time had a voice would
it speak of our decay or
of the rotting fruit at the
feet of where our love
used to lay?

when one belongs
to a yesterday or
understood by a
t o m o r r o w
they are caught
between the has
been and will be…

a today with nowhere to land.

i swallowed the sun

pressed for time

summer faded into fall
and winter came to
remind us we were
never really bare at all
just...

in between tombs
in between blooms
in between the dried
flowers of us hanging
in our rooms.

angie allen

a ghost before
your time
a body lost
a heart beating
on borrowed time.

i swallowed the sun

a warrior's heart finds
its own death, or so
the legend goes, and so
it seems i fell for the
heart of a man dressed
in human clothes

wars waging upon
the land of his skin
battle lines drawn
to protect his strength
within

and yet, i am more
warrior than woman
and i can find my
own death too
and all it took, it seems
was one look inside
of you.

choice is an illusion
the apple hanging
from the tree, the
proverbial trading
of the voice for feet

they don't really want
our voice, so is there a
need to speak when
they only want a
discord played on
repeat?

control is their game
silence their refrain
you try to refrain?
they repeat the chorus

again. and. again.

i swallowed the sun

oh, so you see me do
you, as easy prey?
legs that spread like
the light of day?

i don't need to see you
to *see you*, your words
give you away

it's why i build walls
to keep men like you
away.

ode to jim

would you
press my thigh
see if death
gives us a smile?
we, the soft hour
where clothes fall
between us like
babylon, *swift*
cheeks, *rushed color*
tongues, *velvet*
our paper backs
arched with story.

i swallowed the sun

for as long as i
write about you
you exist here with
me

words on my lips
a soft hour, time forever
braided in our hair.

angie allen

i am mostly made of sundays
looking for my next place of
worship, a place to lay my
hands, a place for the light to
find me...

a place to say *amen.*

i swallowed the sun

writing & you

to come back you
actually have to
go somewhere
and we do, don't we?
there are few things
that bring me back
from where i have
been like writing
and you.

what has the world become, *when we* *speak* silence *like a* *native tongue?*

i swallowed the sun

INTO OBLIVION

intro | into oblivion

2020 will go down in our history books
as one of the most emotionally trying,
politically divisive, and uncharacteristically
insane years modern day history has ever
witnessed. when *covid-19* appeared on
the scene it was a little known virus with ties
to the chinese wet markets. we had no clue
it would turn into a full fledged global
pandemic seemingly overnight. in the days
and weeks to follow we were met with
unprecedented government lockdowns of
entire cities, states, and countries. travel
ceased and bans were put in place. food was
flying off the shelves, some stores deplete of
nearly all essential supplies. our children
were unable to return to school, places of
worship and employment were shut down.
life as we knew it came to a complete stand still.
shelter in place became the new normal as the
world tried to stop the spread of a virus with
no vaccine (or depending on your political
leaning, viable treatments were available if you
had an open mind). those who had the capacity
to work remotely from home did whilst we,
along with our children and families, remained in
doors isolated from others. venturing out was
deemed a necessity and we were required to wear
masks while remaining six feet apart, *social distancing*.

this gave way to frayed emotions and a heightened sense of fear. as a nation we came together briefly united in this shared experience of isolation, only to be ripped apart by the killing of george floyd. what began as peaceful protests quickly escalated into full blown rioting, burning of entire city blocks, destruction and looting of public property, and the toppling of statues and monuments. this morphed into the rise of the *black lives matter* movement which has to date officially rendered the most costly manmade damage to american property in history. as to the unfolding of these events i shall leave to your discernment as the reader to seek out the truth. from my world view when radical ideology began to be offered up to the masses without question reality as we knew it splintered in two. truth became the lie, right became wrong, up became down. it was as if orwell's novel 1984 had walked off the shelves of literary history right into modern day. the poetry that follows was my way of cataloguing the absolute madness we faced, all while still inside of an election year - quite possibly the most important of our republic's history. regardless of the outcome, those of us who collectively experienced these events will always share a unique bond...

we, the survived, have been forever altered.

angie allen

quarantined

and where, i ask, is
the sin, in wanting the
scent of you on my skin?
in wanting to lay heart
to heart? i can't bare much
more of this six feet apart.

mind coup

there is an attempt being made
to rob us blind and take the identity
of us completely from our minds

it's a trojan horse though, you see
that canters under the guise of
e q u a l i t y

it's a mind coup - if you buck the
system they will cancel you

do you mind? yes, yes i do
this is mind over matter and
not matter over mind and i'll
buck against the grain of
insanity every time.

angie allen

churchstate

two independent
ideas should be
s e p a r a t e d
by a period, period.
before they become
too independent.

i swallowed the sun

orwellian

tone deaf, no ring of truth left
media unpersoning the person
until there is no person left
in a state of unable to think
for yourself, never a worry
the plan was always to usher
in doublethink in a hurry
its occupy wall street only
wall street is your mind
in a war led by fear by those
claiming to keep peace
those that are fearless are
truly the free, and well
that just cannot be
when they hold up four fingers
they want you to see three
welcome to the overthrow of
you and of me, and to the entire
democracy - if their new world
order becomes an *ideological
theocracy.*

angie allen

triggered

with hands on the device
they are waiting for outrage
in the land of the violated
and the home of the caved.

i swallowed the sun

something unseen is happening
behind the scenes, behind these
screens and screams of 'fire' in the
streets, burning down entire city
blocks as we speak

justice is a four letter
power play, a trail of ash
left by the clay to usher in
another day

we've been headed towards
another civil war, don't even
know what we're fighting for
people raging against the
machine (the obscene) its
all unseen

something dark is in the now
mobs attacking, people
lacking common sense to
understand there are unseen
forces forcing their hand
unification was never the plan
united was never the stand
we are left with more questions
than when we began.

…line them up in a row

and watch them fall
like dominoes.

19
84

the machine is at it once again
making monsters out of men
what was done to me created
me, echoed the masked man
known as V

line them up in a row and
watch them fall like dominoes
they are creating the very
thing they will destroy, if they
succeed democracy will be
no more

and then we're back to
nineteen eighty fucking four.

i *refuse* to bend a knee
to a modern day theocracy.

i swallowed the sun

there's a new party in town
it hides behind a mask
while burning cities down
it's a colorless machine
that sucks the red from
the blue, destabilizing the US
as it usurps our freedom
and our choices too

whats left of the left is
still not right but hey let's
keep us distracted
so we continue to fight
this machine has become
the new democracy

united in divide i guess
this is war, ever wonder
what we're fighting for?
the lines are getting drawn
in the sand to face our fellow
man, it's civil war once again
while we wonder how we landed
here, in another war lead by fear

p.s. lest we forget this is an election year?

angie allen

*...how's it all
going to* end?

i swallowed the sun

nothing is what it seems
its neo and the matrix
its adam and eve
its the one true man in
the show, they all had to
question what they were
taught to 'know'
and that is how truth begins
when lies bleed out like
questions in your hands
is it the red pill or the blue?
is it the apple or the death to all
you ever thought you knew?

it's a fear of the water because
you might drown but don't you see
the very fear that caged them was
the same fear that set them free
that the only way to freedom was
not to fear the fear at all, they had
to question everything they knew
to get them to…

take the pill, take the bite
take the flight of stairs into
the unknown night

how's it all going to end? well, the
choice is up to you my friend.

angie allen

to follow no one
is to go it alone
a house of skin
with no place to
call home.

let there be light

we are born of
mother earth
we are bound by
father time

we will carry
stories in our
veins of all
the ways that

we survived.

...*and we do come*
back, *don't we?*
even after we fade
to black.

BLACK OUT POETRY

i am *partly*
who i was
who i am
becoming
and who i am
yet to be

this body has
carried the
most of me

these *bones*
have born the
ghosts of me.

i swallowed the sun

i fear my **time**
here has come
to a close and like
carved hearts on
a tree i'll leave
behind **my** poetry
and my **prose.**

angie allen

i'm listening to the rain
fall outside my apartment
window and i think how
beautiful to lose yourself
in pieces to fall and touch
it all

that's what it must be
like to fall into you,
to feel everything i
ever lost come back
to me in

pieces.

i swallowed the sun

i close my eyes and remember when
i could kiss the **sadness** from your skin
i could taste the sunshine of your smile
hold you and forget about life for a while
i miss how your hands always found mine
as we **rocked** on this porch and waved to say hi

your hands were my home, they had **the** kind of
love that knew me, the kind of love that grew me
now you are reduced to **shadows** on this skin that
aches **hollow** where your touch had once been
the sun rises and fades the same all that is left now
is the **taste** of your name

when you left you took the heart **of** me and now
i am but a shell, just a fragile **small** part of me
and yet in **death** i swear it **is** true, this shell of me
still loves the ghost of you

i am sitting here where this house became **home**
in halls that now haunt where true love once roamed
perhaps one day you'll hear us in the wind when
our souls are joined forever **again.**

angie allen

my *body*
bruised
my belly
barren
my hands
empty

my bones are
aching with
i need you
my heart is
echoing *with*
i want you

and yet i always
knew this end*ing*
of me *would be*
the wanting of you.

i never believed in love at first sight
until your words read like memories
at first glance and now these dreams
i dream inside my mind feel more
like memories before their time
it is here between the memory and
the dream where our love flows and
reigns supreme

i will float and dance between the two
until i dream my way back to you
and if i die before i wake i will
find you still make no mistake.

angie allen

low lights
six strings
your tongue
my *name*

whiskey lips
skin bare
my hands
your *hair*

sinful
thoughts
without a
prayer.

you *needed*
to be wanted
i wanted *to be*
needed and we
lived a lifetime
calling it love
now i'm haunted
by the ghost of us
that never truly was.

angie allen

there are **pieces of** us
we carry all tucked away
in the **darkness** of our
minds where the shadows
bleed to grey
yet **memories** don't let
them completely fade away
so we chase their **ghosts**
day, after day, after day
knowing these pieces are
their pieces and with them
we must **play** this game where
moments **chase the memories**
that stay, and stay, and stay.

i swallowed the sun

maybe

i tell myself to stop
wishing on **dead** things
stars that **have lost** their **light**
drowning coins, breaking bones
and **hoping for** the big piece

but 11:11 is always under my tongue
and i save eyelashes just in case
and i wait…and wait….and wait
for the clasp of my necklace to find
my collarbone because i feel it, i just do

you & me unfurling softly like **a maybe.**

angie allen

truth

the greatest
show unearthed
people fear *what*
they do not know
hand them the truth
and they want the show.

190

you *fall out of me*

like leaves
like stars
like rain

things of orchestrated *beauty*
that leave pieces *of themselves*
behind to show they were here
you're not so different and like
them you were never meant to
remain whole, you were *never*
meant to fit in, you were meant
to fall, to flood, to break, to *burn*
how else would the world know you
were here if you didn't leave pieces
of yourself behind? how else could
you share yourself if you didn't shatter
before them? in the *end, it's how i knew*
you were real, in the end *it's how i* knew
you were here

and i… i have the pieces to prove it.

angie allen

before the **earth**
opens her eyes
the light of day
paints her way
and she **smiles**
back **in flowers.**

i see the way
you look at me
all unspoken words
and dark eyes

i look away
before you hear
how i think of you
all slow hands
and vowels.

angie allen

they said i wrote my way **out**
of the **truth** and they could
not have been more correct
albeit, their definition of truth
and mine were **a universe** apart
in the end it was the truth that **set**
me **free**

i lost myself under **a** label
i will never be found under again
and now i walk my own path
just me and this pen and all the
pieces of myself **buried** within

if i had any last **confession** to
make i think it would be

forgive me father for i have **penned.**
p.s. thank you for **the ink.**

forgive me if i
speak **in** petals
the only clothes
i put on my words
is **nature** and if you
undress them **i** think
you'd **find you**r name
has always been here
just spelled a little
differently **each time.**

i have grown quiet
very still and i even
feel time differently
i can taste the
seconds in sunsets

the minutes in stars
the hours in seasons
connected to all that
we were and all we are

yet to be and i realize
this living, this life is a
cocoon and we carry
our wings unseen.

your eyes *saw me*
in a language only
the heart could speak

your words *touched*
me in places hands
could never reach

and admittedly it's
crazy good when a
mind *can* fuck *you*
in ways love never
could.

angie allen

i understand
now what i didn't
know then

the **call** *of* **the**
wild *isn't* **a** *sin*

just a **doorway to**
freedom that lets
the **light** *in.*

i swallowed the sun

flesh and bone
all alone *with no*
one or nothing
to really call home
i *pick up my* **paper**
and **grab** *my pen*
and find my personal
jesus from within.

199

i swallowed the sun

flesh and bone
all alone *with no*
one or nothing
to really call home
i *pick up my* **paper**
and **grab** *my pen*
and find my personal
jesus from within.

angie allen

ronnie

i wish i could tell
you i found **truth**
under rocks and in
sidewalk **cracks**

that i hold **promises**
and dried goodbyes
under **my tongue**

and when the wind
whispers just right **i** still
hear your question
"is there a place
in **heaven** for me?"

well **now** i ask you little
brother, for it is you
telling me.

i *bend over my journal*
to **write** *the same way*
i used **to** *fold my hands*
to **pray** *and the way i*
see it poetry *flowed* **from**
my fingertips *either way.*

Made in the USA
Columbia, SC
29 November 2021

49858830R00114